Matin Latin I

STUDENT'S EDITION

by Karen L. Craig

Illustrated by Laura L. Blakey

Canon Press

MOSCOW, IDAHO

This book is dedicated to
Charles, God's gift of love in human form;
Darol, God's gift of encouragement;
David, God's gift of living sunshine.

Special Thanks to Deb and Donna, amīcae fīdae
and proofreaders extraordinaire,
to the Blakey family, to Tora and Kim,
and to all my young students who struggled with
me through adaptations of "bid kids" texts.

Karen L. Craig, *Matin Latin 1 (Student's Edition)*

©1999 by Karen L. Craig
Published by Canon Press, P.O. Box 8741, Moscow, ID 83843
800-488-2034

Illustrations by Laura L. Blakey
Cover Design by Paige Atwood Design, Moscow, ID

Printed in the United States of America

ISBN: 1-885767-46-3

Matin Latin I

Table of Contents

Why Latin for Young Children?

Young children and their parents are challenged by the lack of age-appropriate texts for studying Latin. The scope and sequence of this text is drawn from my study and experiences in teaching Latin, French, and English in classroom, homeschool, and tutorial settings. Rote memory is an integral part of the course. Young children thrive on learning lists! Practical application of the memory work in sentences and stories serves to encourage more memory work. This text combines the grammar necessary to read stories early in the study of Latin with the usual work on Latin endings. Latin has five declensions of nouns and four conjugations of verbs. English has one declension and many exceptions to the declension rules. This text teaches only one declension of nouns and one conjugation of verbs (in three tenses, not all six!). Even within these limits there are many stories a child will enjoy, much as a young reader of English is limited, at first, to one-syllable words, yet has great delight in these stories. For pre-readers, the beauty of this text is that it allows the students to draw pictures to express comprehension and to give oral sentences from pictures in the text.

Since the study of a language is for the purpose of being able to read, write, and communicate in *that* language, pictures (concepts) are used to define the Latin words. A picture of a girl means the same thing to anyone who sees it, no matter which word they would use to describe the picture in their native tongue. For this reason, a student who can draw a picture which represents the Latin sentence is farther along the road to understanding what he reads than a student who must translate each word individually to English.

Pronunciation

There is some debate about the value of learning a Latin pronunciation.[1] Since we have no "native" speakers of Classical Latin, an exact oral standard is not available. Until recently when Latin has been reinstated in some public school systems as part of multicultural education, it was taught as a written and read language. Even when the primary purpose of the course is the reading of Latin, oral work proves very useful. I offer a standard classical Latin pronunciation chart for four reasons. First, Latin pronunciation is much simpler than English because each vowel has only two sounds, long or short! The consonants, also, have only one sound each. Second, in the event that a student continues Latin study to the point of reading poetry, he will already have the pronunciation rules essential to good reading of Latin poetry. Third, pronunciation and diacritical marks (macrons and accents) are an essential part of many modern languages. Fourth, holding to a standard pronunciation eases the transition of study with different teachers and in different geographic locations.

---

[1] Douglas Wilson, "The Why and How of Latin," *Repairing the Ruins*, ed. Douglas Wilson (Moscow ID: Canon Press, 1996), pp. 133-145.

An alphabetic phonics chart looks like this (to alleviate pronunciation difficulties, in the English examples phonetic symbols from Webster's New Collegiate Dictionary were used):

Vowels					
Long	Latin	English	Short	Latin	English
ā	irāta, lāta	father	a	casa	banana, but
ē	poēta, rēs, tē	date, day, they	e	et, est	bet, met
ī	prīma, vīlla	beet, easy	i	in, inter	in, pin
ō	Rōma, sōla	bone, no	o	bona, nova	obey, omit
(ō and o are very similar)					
ū	fortūna, lacūna	food, loot, lute	u	sub, sunt	foot, full, put
Diphthongs					
ae	puellae, tubae	aisle, eye			
au	aut, nauta	out, pouch			
(Infrequent dipthongs are included here only for reference: <u>ei</u> as in n<u>ei</u>ghbor and w<u>ei</u>gh; <u>oe</u> as in <u>oy</u> in b<u>oy</u>, j<u>oy</u>; <u>eu</u> as in f<u>eu</u>d, and f<u>ew</u>; <u>ui</u> as in q<u>ue</u>en.)					

Consonants			
b, d, f, h, k, l, m, n, p, qu, r sound the same in Latin and in English		s	as in *say*
bs and bt	have a soft sound like *ps* and *pt*	t	as in *ton*
c and ch	always hard as in *character*	th	as in *thyme* or *thick* (not as in *then*)
g	always hard as in *go*	ti	as in *tin* (does **not** combine as in *nation*)
gu	as in *anguish*	v	always sounds like *w* as in *wall*
i (j)	begins a word and is followed by a vowel; sounds like *y* in *yam*	x	always sounds like *ks* as in *axe* (double consonant)
ph	as in *photograph*	z	always sounds like *dz* as in *adze* (double consonant)

The syllabication of Latin words

Dividing into syllables and placing an accent makes a word easier to pronounce.

    A. Each vowel or diphthong has its own syllable.

    B. Consonants are pronounced with the following vowel. Two consonants are divided and one pronounced with each vowel.

    C. Consonant blends: *h, l,* and *r* combine with a preceding *c, g, p, b, d,* or *t* to form a blend which is pronounced with the following vowel.

    D. When *u* follows *g, q,* and sometimes *s,* it sounds like *w* and forms a blend which is pronounced with the following vowel.

    E. Double consonants: *x* is pronounced with the preceding vowel, *z* is pronounced with the following vowel.

    F. The last syllable of a Latin word is the *ultima,* the next to last is the *penult,* and the one before that is the *antepenult.*

Accents

In words of more than one syllable, the ultima is never accented. (*This rule is ignored during Practice Chants.*) If the penult is long (it has a long vowel or is followed by two or more consonants), it is accented. If the penult is short, the accent will be on the antepenult. Simply stated, *if the next to last syllable is long, it is accented. If the next to last syllable is short, the syllable which precedes it receives the accent.* For your convenience, vocabulary lists in this text have the syllables divided and the accents marked.

Lesson One

In order to study a new language like Latin, a person must have a good understanding of the basics of his own language. In this book, we will learn how words fit together to make good sentences in English and Latin.

A noun is the name of a person, place, thing, or idea. *Girl, boy, forest, water,* and *friendship* are all nouns. Can you name some other nouns?

Nouns which tell who or what is doing the action of the sentence are called *subject* nouns, or the *subject* of the sentence.

To help you remember the noun rule, sing this song to the tune of *London Bridge is Falling Down:*

A noun names a
Person (Pers'n), place thing,
Pers'n, place, thing,
Pers'n, place, thing.
A noun names a
    pers'n, place, thing,
Like LAD and LADY!

Lesson One Exercises

A. Underline the subject nouns in these sentences.

   1. The sailors sail.

   2. The girls walk.

   3. Women call.

   4. Farmers work.

   5. A poet tells.

   6. Pirates and sailors sail.

   7. Maids work.

   8. Julia and I sing.

   9. The picture is pretty.

   10. The pirates stand.

Lesson Two

Latin nouns change their form (the way they look) depending on their function (what they do) in a sentence. In a vocabulary list, the first form shown is the form which is used for the subject noun in a sentence. This form is called the nominative case. Learn the complete entry for each word. For example: *puella, -ae, f. – girl,* is the complete entry for the Latin word that means *girl. Puella* is the form we use for the singular subject noun of the sentence. This form is called the *nominative case. Puellae,* the second form, is called the *genitive case.* We use it to find the stem to which we add the other case endings. We will learn its other uses later.

Here is the complete paradigm (chart or chant) for the noun *puella*.

CASE	SINGULAR	PLURAL
Nominative	puella	puellae
Genitive	puellae	puellārum
Dative	puellae	puellīs
Accusative	puellam	puellās
Ablative	puellā	puellīs

a GRI co la, -ae, m.

A mi ta, -ae, f.

FA mu la, -ae, f.

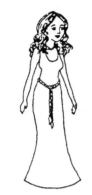

FĒ mi na, -ae, f.

IN co la, -ae, m.

pu EL la, -ae, f.

You see that some of the vocabulary words are followed by *f.* and some by *m.* These letters stand for *feminine* and *masculine.* Every Latin noun has a gender (masculine, feminine, or neuter). These do not mean the exact same thing as a boy, a girl, and a thing, as they do in English. Learn the gender with the noun and later we will learn how the gender is important.

Lesson Two Exercises

A. Chant the noun paradigm each day this week. Use the new vocabulary words. Make an X over each day that you do the chant.

Monday   Tuesday   Wednesday   Thursday   Friday

B. Answer these questions with a Latin word.

1. To talk about a farmer, which Latin word would we use?
2. To talk about maids, which Latin word would we use?
3. To talk about a settler, which Latin word would we use?
4. To talk about girls, which Latin word would we use?
5. To talk about aunts, which Latin word would we use?

Lesson Three

A pronoun is a short word which takes the place of a noun. Words like *I, you, he, she, it, we, you, they* are subject pronouns. We talk about these pronouns as *first person, second person,* and *third person* pronouns. If we talk about one person, we use a *singular* pronoun. If we talk about more than one person, we use a *plural* pronoun. But what does *first person, second person, third person* mean? This idea is easier to understand if we draw a picture.

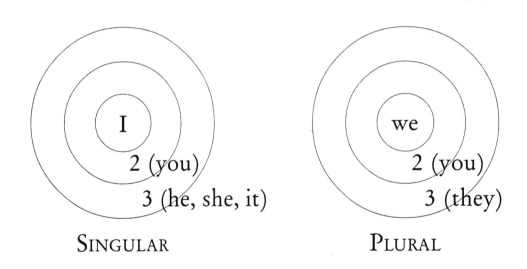

SINGULAR   PLURAL

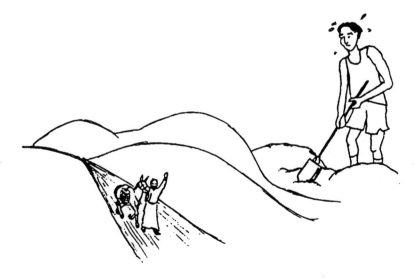

Lesson Three Exercises

A. In the following groups of words, choose a subject pronoun to replace the subject noun(s).

   1. The sailors sail.   _____ sail.

   2. A poet tells.   _____ tells.

   3. Women call.   _____ call.

   4. Farmers work.   _____ work.

   5. Pam and Ann walk.   _____ walk.

   6. George and I call.   _____ call.

   7. You and Jane tell.   _____ tell.

   8. Sally carries.   _____ carries.

   9. The cat walks.   _____ walks.

 10. Animals run.   _____ run.

B. Now tell whether the pronouns are first, second, or third person, singular or plural.

Lesson Four

A verb is an action word. It tells what the noun or pronoun does. *Run, walk, call, sing, work,* and *tell* are verbs.

Lesson Four Exercises

A. Underline the verbs with a red crayon.

1. The woman tells.

2. A girl watches.

3. Settlers are exploring.

4. The farmers walk.

5. She wanders.

6. Janet and John carry.

7. God loves.

8. Jeremiah preaches.

9. Noah builds.

10. The machine is working.

To help you remember the verb rule, sing this song to the tune of *Row, Row, Row Your Boat.*

Verbs are action words,
Verbs are action words,
Ve-rbs a-re action wo-rds,
LIVE and LOVE and LEARN!

Lesson Five

In Latin we will learn about nouns, pronouns, and verbs. The interesting thing about Latin is that pronouns are shown by the ending on the verb! This means that we can look at a verb and tell what is the subject pronoun.

The chart below shows which verb ending (or personal ending) is used for each pronoun.

	SINGULAR (one)	PLURAL (more than one)
1st Person	vocō—*I call*	vocāmus—*we call*
2nd Person	vocās—*you call*	vocātis—*you (pl.) call*
3rd Person	vocat—*he, she, it calls*	vocant—*they call*

Thinking about a verb in this way is called conjugating. When we conjugate a verb, we tell (or write) how it would look if we talked about all the subject pronouns. By putting them in a chart it is easier to remember them later. When we say these words or endings in order, it sounds like a chant. That is why sometimes the charts we learn in Latin are called chants.

Lesson Five Exercises

A. Give the person (first, second, or third) and number (singular or plural) of the subject pronoun(s) in these sentences. Unless a pronoun has the plural marker, (pl.), it is singular.

1. He praises.
2. They watch.
3. She wanders.
4. I shout.
5. We call.
6. You carry.
7. It sails.
8. You (pl.) praise.
9. He is singing.
10. We do pray.

Challenge:

11. He and I watch.
12. He and she are singing.

B. Here are some Latin verbs for which you do not know the meaning. Study the verb chart in this lesson. Then tell the person and number of each subject pronoun. Ex: Vocō 1S

1. Laudat.
2. Amō.
3. Clamās.
4. Dant.
5. Stātis.
6. Ambulat.
7. Conservat.
8. Vocāmus.
9. Cēlās.
10. Spectātis.
11. Rogat.
12. Orant.
13. Explōrō.
14. Monstrāmus.

C. Chant the verb paradigm using a different verb each day.
Monday   Tuesday   Wednesday   Thursday   Friday

Lesson Six

A Latin verb tells us two things: *who* did the action (the subject pronoun) and *when* the action was done. *When an action happened* is called the *tense* (or time) of the verb.

When we talk about what someone is doing now, or today, we are talking about what is happening in the present time. In Latin, we call this form of the verb the *present tense.*

To make a present tense verb in Latin, we find the verb's present stem. Look at *vocō, vocāre, vocāvī, vocātum.* These are called the four principal parts of the verb because they are the most important parts and other parts can be made from them. The first principal part, *vocō,* tells how our present tense chart begins. Now look at the second principal part, *vocāre.* This part is also called the *infinitive* and it means *to call.* To find the present stem so that we can complete our chart, however, we must change this part to *vocā* by dropping the *-re* from it. *Vocā* is the *present stem* of this verb.

Infinitive – *re* = Present stem

After we have found the present stem it is easy to form the complete chant. To the present stem, add the personal endings (*-ō, -s, -t, -mus, -tis, -nt*). In your vocabulary list, you will notice that all the verbs have four parts. Memorize all the four parts, but we will be using only the first two parts at this time.

Present stem + personal endings = present tense

Lesson Six Exercises

A. To practice using the first two parts of a verb, answer these questions.

1. Which part of the verb would we use to say *to call*?

2. Which part of the verb says *I call* ?

3. If we are doing something right now, what tense will we use to conjugate the verb?

4. What are the personal endings for the present tense?

5. How would we say *I am calling? You (pl) are calling? It calls?*

Lesson Seven

With the information you have learned, you are now able to read Latin sentences. It is important that you understand the meaning of the sentences, just as you do when reading English. Think about the pictures that the sentences are painting, instead of what the sentence would look like in English words.

Lesson Seven Exercises

A. Study this new vocabulary. Remember to learn the entire Latin entry for each word.

BĒS ti a, -ae, f. CA sa, -ae, f. FĪ li a, -ae, f.

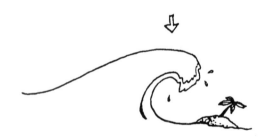

UN da, -ae, f. UR sa, -ae, f.

AM bu lō, -āre, -āvī, -ātum A mō, -āre, -āvī, -ātum

ap pro PIN quō, -āre, -āvī, -ātum

CLA mō, -āre, -āvī, -ātum

LA bō rō, -āre, -āvī, -ātum

VO cō, -āre, -āvī, -ātum

B. Read these Latin sentences. Draw a picture to show their meaing.

1. Agricola ambulat.   2. Unda appropinquat.

3. Bēstia vocat.   4. Agricola labōrat.

5. Fēmina labōrat.   6. Incola vocat.

7. Fīlia clamat.

8. Amita ambulat.

9. Agricolae labōrant.

10. Ursa appropinquat.

11. Amō.

For sentences like this you may want
to use a number or letter to show the
subject pronoun. (Ex. 1S)

12. Vocās.

13. Clamat.   14. Ambulāmus.

C. Each day this week, practice your noun chant using a different noun each day. Cross out the day when you have finished the chant.

   Monday   Tuesday   Wednesday   Thursday   Friday

D. Each day this week, practice your verb chant using a different verb each day. Cross out the day when you have finished the chant.

   Monday   Tuesday   Wednesday   Thursday   Friday

Just for Fun

Incola labōrat. Agricola labōrat. Fēmina et (and) amita ambulant. Fīlia et famula ambulant. Bēstia appropinquat. Fēmina vocat. Agricola clamat. Fīlia nōn (not) appropinquat!

Lesson Eight

There is a special verb in Latin which has its very own chant. This verb is called a "state of being" verb. We have it in English, too. First, we will learn the chant. Then we will learn how to use this verb. The four principal parts of this verb are *sum, esse, fuī, futūrum*.

This is what the *sum* chant looks like:

Singular	Plural
sum—I am	*sumus*—we are
es—you are	*estis*—you (pl.) are
est—he, she, it is	*sunt*—they are

When this verb begins a sentence it means *it is*, *there is*, or *they are*, *there are*.

For example: *Est casa* tells us there is a house.

Sunt amitae tells us there are aunts.

Lesson Eight Exercises

A. Say (or write) the following ideas in Latin. Ex: I am a farmer.
Agricola sum.

1. You are a settler.   _____

2. She is an aunt.   _____

3. We are maids.   _____

4. You (pl.) are women.   _____

5. They are farmers.   _____

6. There is a beast.   _____

7. It is a girl.   _____

8. There are cottages.   _____

9. There is a settler.   _____

10. There are maids.   _____

11. They are girls.   _____

12. There is a farmer.   _____

B. Chant the *sum* chant, a noun chant, and a regular verb chant each day. Give yourself a star for each day that you do all three.

Monday   Tuesday   Wednesday   Thursday   Friday

C. Write some original Latin sentences.

_____

_____

_____

_____

_____

_____

_____

_____

_____

_____

_____

_____

_____

_____

_____

_____

_____

Lesson Nine

When the verb in the predicate is *to be* (*is* or *are*), it is called a "linking verb" because it links two things that are the same. In these sentences, the noun after the linking verb is called a predicate nominative.

Remember that the subject noun names what the sentence is about. The predicate of the sentence tells what the subject noun is or does. The predicate nominative is a noun in the predicate that renames the subject noun. Look at a few English sentences that show this idea.

A. The girl is a maid.

The girl is the subject. *Is a maid* is the predicate; it tells about *the girl. Maid* is the predicate nominative. It is the noun in the predicate that renames the subject noun.

B. The woman is my aunt.

The woman is the subject; *woman* is the subject noun. *Is my aunt* is the predicate; *is* is the linking verb and *aunt* is the predicate nominative.

C. The settlers are farmers.

The settlers is the subject, *are* is the linking verb, and *farmers* is the predicate nominative.

Lesson Nine Exercises

A. Tell (or label with blue crayon) the subject noun (S) and the predicate nominative (PN) in each of these sentences. *Note:* A person's name counts as one noun.

1. The man was a president.
2. Noah was a carpenter.
3. Jim is a student.
4. Nan is a girl.
5. Stuart Little was a mouse.
6. Daniel Boone was a hunter.
7. Columbus was an explorer.
8. That lady is my mother.
9. The boys are his sons.
10. The children are blessings.

Challenge sentences:

11. My loving father is a hard worker.
12. The tired sailors became happy farmers.
13. Every day is a new beginning.
14. The cheerful little boy was a great helper.
15. Daniel was a servant of the true God.

Lesson Ten

In Latin when the verb *sum* links two nouns in a sentence, it is called a "'linking verb" because it links two things that are the same. The subject noun and the predicate nominative are both in the nominative case because they name the same thing.

A. Puella est famula.

Puella is the subject noun, *est* is the linking verb, and *famula* is the predicate nominative. The sentence would mean the same thing if we wrote it backwards: *Famula est puella.*

B. Fēmina est amita.

Fēmina is the subject noun, *est* is the linking verb, and *amita* is the predicate nominative. We could also say: *Amita est fēmina.*

C. Incolae sunt agricolae.

Incolae is the subject noun, *sunt* is the linking verb, and *agricolae* is the predicate nominative. Notice the *agricolae* is nominative plural. It renames *incolae* which is also plural. *Sunt* is a plural verb because it has a plural subject noun. We could also say: *Agricolae sunt incolae.*

Lesson Ten Exercises

A. Study this new vocabulary. Remember to learn the entire Latin entry for each word.

A qua, -ae, f.   Ā ra, -ae, f.   FĀ bu la, -ae, f.

FĀ ma, -ae, f.   ha RĒ na, -ae, f.   MEN sa, -ae, f.

NAU ta, -ae, m.   po Ē ta, -ae, m.   RĪ pa, -ae, f.

B. Say or write a good Latin sentence for each of these pictures.

1.

2.

_____   _____

3.

4.

_____   _____

5.

_____

C. Chant the *sum* chant, a noun chant, and a regular verb chant each day. Give yourself a star if you choose a differnt verb each day.

Monday	Tuesday	Wednesday	Thursday	Friday
sum __	sum __	sum __	sum __	sum __
noun __	noun __	noun __	noun __	noun __
verb __	verb __	verb __	verb __	verb __

D. Now write some of your own Latin sentences. Use many plural subject nouns.

_____

_____

_____

_____

_____

_____

_____

_____

_____

_____

_____

_____

Just for Fun

Singing is a good way to learn lots of things. Here are songs you may already know. Practice them until they are as easy to sing in Latin as they are in English!

America[1]
Tē canō, Patria,
Candida, lībera,
Tē referet.
Portus et exulum
Et tumulus senum;
Lībera montium
Vōx resonet.

Jesus Loves Me[2]
Christus mē amat,
His sciō.
Quod Scriptūra hunc nārrat.
Līberī ad eum sunt.
Dēfessī sunt, sed firmus est.
Christus mē amat,
Christus mē amat,
Christus mē amat,
Scriptūra hunc nārrat.

[1] Latin version by Professor George D. Kellogg.
[2] Latin version by Karen L. Craig.

Lesson Eleven

Sometimes we want to talk about what someone used to do, or what he was doing before today. Then we are talking about what was happening in the past time. In English this tense is called the *past tense* or the *simple past tense.* In Latin, we call this the *imperfect tense.* Remember that the imperfect tense tells about past action that was not completed all at once. It was a habit or an action that took place over a period of time.

On a timeline, it might look like this:

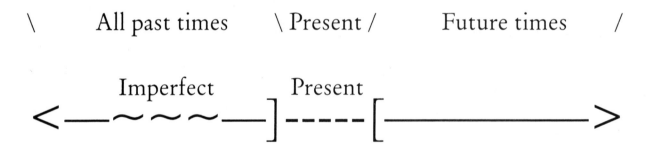

Lesson Eleven Exercises

A. Tell (or write with red crayon) the tense (present or imperfect) for the verbs.

1. Androcles serves a Roman master. _____

2. He was hiding in a cave. _____

3. A lion comes into the cave. _____

4. Androcles does not move. _____

5. The lion shows a thorn in his foot. _____

6. Quickly the slave removes the thorn. _____

7. Then the lion and the slave were living in the cave together for a long time. _____

8. But the Roman finds his slave. _____

9. He sends Androcles to the lions in the arena. _____

10. The lion was remembering his friend. _____

11. The emperor frees the brave man. _____

12. The lion and the man were living happily. _____

Lesson Twelve

To make an imperfect tense verb in Latin, we fing the verb's present stem (the second principal part minus the -*re*). Then we add a tence sign (*bā*) and the personal endings (-*ō* [or *m*], -*s*, -*t*, -*mus*, -*tis*, -*nt*) to it.

Present stem + bā + personal endings = Imperfect tense

This is the chant chart for the imperfect tense:

SINGULAR	PLURAL
vocābam—*I was calling, I used to call*	vocābāmus—*we were calling*
vocābās—*you were calling*	vocābātis—*you (pl.) were calling*
vocābat—*he, she, it was calling*	vocābant—*they were calling*

Lesson Twelve Exercises

A. Study this new vocabulary. Remember to learn the entire Latin entry for each word.

CĒ lō -āre, -āvī, -ātum

ER rō, -āre, -āvī, -ātum

ex PEC tō, -āre, -āvī, -ātum

ex PLŌ rō, -āre, -āvī, -ātum

HA bi tō, -āre, -āvī, -ātum

IU vō, -āre, iūvī, iūtum

LAU dō, -āre, -āvī, -ātum

MU tō, -āre, āvī, ātum

NĀR rō, -āre, -āvī, -ātum

NĀ vi gō, -āre, -āvī, -ātum

B. Read these Latin sentences. Draw a picture to show their meaning.

   1. Agricola ambulābat.   2. Amita expectābat.

3. Bēstia mutābat.

4. Agricola laudābat.

5. Fēmina laborābat.

6. Incola explōrābat.

7. Fīlia cēlābat.

8. Amita errābat.

9. Agricolae expectābant.   10. Bēstiae appropinquābant.

11. Habitābam.   12. Iuvābās.

13. Clamābat.   14. Nārrābāmus.

15. Nāvigābātis.   16. Labōrābant.

C. Choose five of the verbs from this list. Write their four principle parts below. Conjugate (say the chant for) them in the present and imperfect tenses.

_____

_____

_____

_____

_____

Lesson Thirteen

Sometimes we want to talk about what someone will do after today. Then we are talking about what will happen in the future time (tomorrow, or after that). We call this the *future tense*.

Review:

When we talk about what is happening now, we use the present tense.

When we talk about what used to happen or what was happening, we use the imperfect tense.

Lesson Thirteen Exercises

A. Give the tense of the verb (present, imperfect, future) for each sentence.

1. Joshua was a brave man.
2. He was leading the children of Israel.
3. Jericho is a wicked city.
4. Joshua wants to take the city.
5. Joshua and the people will march around the city for seven days.
6. The seventh day they were marching.
7. The trumpets of the priests are blowing.
8. The people shout.
9. The walls of Jericho are falling.
10. Now the children of Israel will travel on.

B. Chant or write the *sum* chant five times.

C. Chant the noun chant for these nouns:
    aqua   *fāma*   *bēstia*   *fēmina*

D. Write your own sentences. Use many plural verbs. Write with a purple pencil!

_____

_____

_____

_____

_____

_____

_____

_____

_____

Lesson Fourteen

In Latin we have the future tense also. The future tense tells about action that will happen sometime after now . . . in the future. On a timeline, it would look like this:

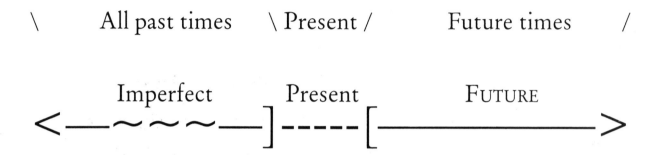

To make a future tense verb in Latin, we find the verb's present stem (the second principal part minus the *-re*). Then we add a tense sign (*bi*) and the personal endings (*-ō, -s, -t, -mus, -tis, -nt*) to it.

> Present stem + bi + personal endings =
> Future tense

This is the chant chart for the future tense:

SINGULAR	PLURAL
vocābō—I will call	*vocābimus*—we will call
vocābis—you will call	*vocābitis*—you (pl.) will call
vocābit—he, she, it will call	*vocābunt*—they will call

Review:

PRESENT TENSE		IMPERFECT TENSE	
vocō	vocāmus	vocābam	vocābāmus
vocās	vocātis	vocābās	vocābātis
vocat	vocant	vocābat	vocābant

Lesson Fourteen Exercises

A. Study this new vocabulary. Remember to learn the entire Latin entry for each word.

HAS ta, -ae, f.   NYM pha, -ae, f.   pī RĀ ta, -ae, m.

NE cō, -āre, -āvī, -ātum   NŌ mi nō, -āre, -āvī, -ātum

OC cu pō, -āre, -āvī, -ātum   Ō rō, -āre, -āvī, -ātum

op PUG nō, -āre, -āvī, -ātum

POS tu lō, -āre, -āvī, ātum

POR tō, -āre, -āvī, -ātum

PRO pe rō, -āre, -āvī, -ātum

B. Read each Latin sentence. Draw a picture or write a sentence to show meaning.

1. Hastae necābunt.   2. Nauta ōrābit.

3. Nympha nōminābit.   4. Incolae occupābunt.

5. Pīrātae oppugnābunt.   6. Poēta properābit.

7. Portābō.   8. Postulābis.

9. Nōminābit.   10. Occupābimus.

11. Ōrābitis.   12. Oppugnābunt.

13. Pīrāta cēlābit.   14. Poēta errābit.

Lesson Fifteen

The verb *sum* has an imperfect tense and a future tense also.
They look like this:

IMPERFECT

SINGULAR   PLURAL

eram—I was   *erāmus*—we were
erās—you were   *erātis*—you (pl.) were
erat—he, she, it was   *erant*—they were

FUTURE

SINGULAR   PLURAL

erō—I shall be   *erimus*—we shall be
eris—you will be   *eritis*—you (pl.) will be
erit—he, she, it will be   *erunt*—they will be

Lesson Fifteen Exercises

A. Study this new vocabulary. Remember to learn the entire Latin entry for each word.

co RŌ na, -ae, f.   CO ma, -ae, f.   CŪ ra, -ae, f.

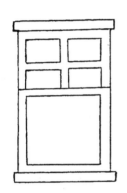 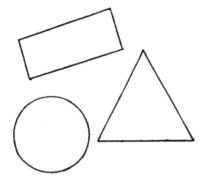 

fe NES tra, -ae, f.   fi GŪ ra, -ae, f.   FLAM ma, -ae, f.

GA le a, -ae, f.   GEM ma, -ae, f.

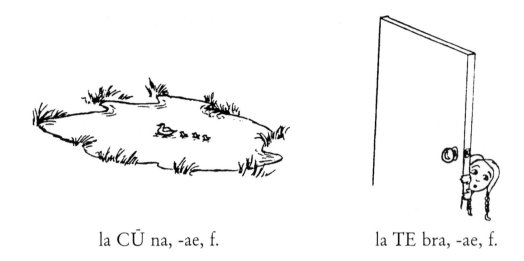

la CŪ na, -ae, f.   la TE bra, -ae, f.

B. Read these sentences. Draw a picture or write a sentence to show the meaning. You may want to use an = sign for the linking verb.

1. Coma erat corōna.   2. Galea erit gemma.

3. Incolae erant agricolae.   4. Fēmina erit famula.

5. Fēmina est amita.

6. Puellae erunt fīliae.

7. Nautae erunt poētae.

8. Mensa est āra.

9. Fābulae sunt fāmae.

10. Fīlia erat nympha.

11. Pīrātae erunt agricolae.   12. Fīliae erant fēminae.

13. Nauta erat pīrāta.   14. Nautae erunt incolae.

C. Chant the three tenses of the verb *sum*.
    Present
    Imperfect
    Future

D. Chant the noun paradigm for each of these nouns from Exercise A.

co RŌ na

CO ma

fe NES tra

GEM ma

la CŪ na

Just for Fun

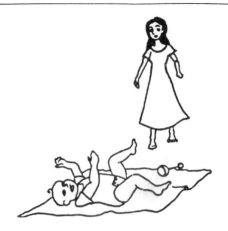

Herī (yesterday) Iulia erat puella. Iulia nōn ambulābat. Iulia nōn explōrābat. Clamābat. Fēmina appropinquābat.

Hodiē (today) Iulia est puella. Amita et Iulia ambulant et explōrant. Amita et Iulia labōrant. Amant nāvigare.

Crās (tomorrow) Iulia erit fēmina. Lucus et Iulia ambulābunt. Explōrābunt. Nāvigabunt. Amābunt amāre.

Lesson Sixteen

We learned to tell about the action of a subject. We can even make simple statements about a thing. (The farmer walks. The dog is running.) But to make our sentences and stories interesting, we may add another noun after the action verb. This noun is called the *direct object noun* and it tells *who* or *what* received the action of the verb.

> ### To find the direct object, ask:
> ### "Who or what received the action?"

Look at these sentences.

A. The sailor sails a ship.

Sailor is the subject noun, *sails* is the verb (tells the action of the subject noun), and *ship* is the direct object noun (tells *what* the sailor sails).

B. The girls tell many stories.

Girls is the subject noun, *tell* is the verb, and *stories* is the direct object noun.

C. The pirates were capturing settlers.

Pirates is the subject noun, *were capturing* is the verb, and *settlers* is the direct object noun.

> To help you remember the noun rule, sing this song to the tune of *B-I-N-G-O:*
>
> Oh, once a farmer had a dog;
> And D.O. was his name, oh!
> Dog is the D.O.
> Dog is the D.O.
> Dog is the D.O.
> It's WHAT the farmer had!

Lesson Sixteen Exercises

A. Give the subject noun (or pronoun), the verb, and the direct object for each sentence. There will be extra words in some sentences. These are not important for now. (These sentences come from a myth told by the Romans and the Greeks to explain the creation of frogs.)

1. The ancient Greeks saw goddesses.
2. They saw goddesses in the forests, not in fields.
3. Latona had many altars in the forests of Greece. (Latona was a goddess.)
4. The small daughter of Latona sees a pool.
5. She wants some good water.
6. Latona begs water from the nearby farmers.
7. The farmers tell a false story about the water.
8. They do not give water to Diana.
9. Angry Latona curses the farmers.
10. "Now you have houses to live in.
11. Soon the water in the pool will have frogs."
12. Suddenly the lying men had four legs!
13. They had a pool of water for their home.
14. Some people still believe these myths.
15. Do you believe myths?

B. Tell the sentence pattern (S-LV-PN or S-V-DO) for these sentences.

1. At first Rome did not have good water.

2. The well-water was dirty water.

3. Only small cisterns held good water.

4. Aqueducts carried much good water from the mountains outside Rome.

5. In the city, the first aqueduct was an underground pipe.

6. The huge sewers of Rome were also underground tunnels.

7. In the United States, some cities have aqueducts to carry good water.

8. These aqueducts are big, long pipes.

9. Many cities in the United States have large underground sewers.

10. Do aqueducts supply water for your home?

Lesson Seventeen

In Latin direct object nouns are easy to tell apart from subject nouns and predicate nominatives. Direct object nouns use the *accusative* case.

Look again at the paradigm chart. We have learned the uses for the nominative case. Now we will learn a use for the *accusative* case.

CASE	SINGULAR	PLURAL
Nominative	puella	puellae
Genitive	puellae	puellārum
Dative	puellae	puellīs
Accusative	puellam	puellās
Ablative	puellā	puellīs

Look at the following examples of S-V-DO sentences. You will see that the word order is not the same as it would be in English. Very soon this new word order will be comfortable for you.

A. Agricola fēminam amat.

Agricola is the subject noun, *fēminam* is the direct object noun, and *amat* is the verb.

B. Famula fābulam nārrat.

Famula is the subject noun, *fābulam* is the direct object noun, and *nārrat* is the verb.

C. Fīliae gemmās cēlābant.

This sentence has a plural subject noun: *fīliae;* a plural direct object noun: *gemmās;* and a plural verb (to agree with its plural subject): *cēlābant.*

Lesson Seventeen Exercises

A. Study this new vocabulary. Remember to learn the entire Latin entry for each word.

HER ba, -ae, f.   ĪN su la, -ae, f.   IĀ nu a, -ae, f.

nā VI cu la, -ae, f.   RĒ gi a, -ae, f.   rē GĪ na, -ae, f.

Ō ra, -ae, f.   pae NĪN su la, -ae, f.   prō VIN ci a, -ae, f.

B. Read the sentences below. Draw a picture to show the meaning.

1. Rēgīna rēgiam habitat.   2. Incolae īnsulam explōrābat.

3. Ursa amitam appropinquābit.   4. Rēgīnae corōnās ōrant.

5. Agricola bēstiās necābat.   6. Puellam vocāmus.

7. Gemmās cēlābitis.   8. Fēmina casam postulābant.

9. Aquae rīpās mutant.   10. Pīrātae hastās et galeās
portābant.

11. Nauta nāviculam
nāvigat.   12. Incolae prōvinciam laudant.

13. Fīlia fābulās amat nārrāre.

14. Undae nautās iuvābant.

15. Pīrāta casam oppugnat.

16. Pīrātae sumus.

17. Mensam ōrābitis.

18. Bēstiae herbās expectant.

C. Add the correct endings to the words in these sentences.
Look carefully. There are three kinds of nouns: subject, direct
object, predicate nominative.

1. Nympha agricol____ appropinquat.
2. Naut____ curās nōn expectant. (nōn=*not*)
3. Nāvicula fēmin____ portābat.
4. Incola fīli____ (more than one) nōminābit.
5. Paenīnsula īnsul____ nōn est.
6. Rēgīna rēgi____ habitābat.
7. Ōra harēn____ est.
8. Figūrae iānu____ sunt.
9. Amit____ nōn sumus.
10. Pīrātae agricol____ (plural) nōn iuvābunt.

D. Write the four principal parts of these verbs, then chant the present, imperfect, and future chants for each one.

Labōrō _____

Portō _____

Cēlō _____

Ambulō _____

Laudō _____

E. Write an interesting paragraph in English. Use three verb tenses. Underline the linking verbs; circle the action verbs.

_____

_____

_____

_____

_____

_____

_____

_____

_____

Lesson Eighteen

When we want to tell about something that belongs to someone, or what someone or something has, we use a possessive
noun. Here are some examples:

    John's hat

    the girl's coat

    the man's rabbit

John's, girl's and *man's* are all possessive nouns.

Sometimes we use a group of words to show this idea of possession. Look at the following examples:

    It is the rim *of the wheel*.

    It is the door *of the house*.

Both of these sentences show possession. The wheel has a rim
and the house has a door. It would be correct (but not as smooth
sounding) to say *the wheel's rim* or *the house's door*.

Lesson Eighteen Exercises

A. Underline the phrase (group of words) or the noun which shows possession.

1. Daniel was a slave of Babylon.

2. He was with God's other servants.

3. He did not eat the king's food.

4. Advisors of the king did not like Daniel.

5. They did not like Daniel's prayers.

6. The men kept a den of lions.

7. The king was tricked into agreeing to the men's wicked plan.

8. When Daniel prayed at the window of his room, they took him away.

9. The lion's den was a safe place for Daniel.

10. The angel of the Lord kept Daniel safe.

Lesson Nineteen

In Latin, we have possessive noun, too. When we use the possessive form of nouns in English, we add *'s* or a phrase beginning with *of*. In Latin the possessive form is called the *genitive case*. It also makes a change in the way the noun looks. Look at the noun paradigm. The genitive ending for a singular noun is *-ae*. The genitive for a plural noun is *-ārum*.

CASE	SINGULAR	PLURAL
Nominative	puella	puellae
Genitive	puellae	puellārum
Dative	puellae	puellīs
Accusative	puellam	puellās
Ablative	puellā	puellīs

To tell about the girl's aunt walking, we would say *Amita puellae ambulat.* In this example, *amita* is in the nominative case because it is the subject of the sentence. *Puellae* is in the genitive case because it tells whose aunt. Generally, in Latin the genitive case noun comes directly after the noun it modifies (tells about). Look at the following examples:

    A. Famula rēgīnae laborat.

Famula is the subject noun and *rēgīnae* is the possessive noun.

B. Gemmae rēgīnae cēlābant.

Gemmae is the plural subject noun. *Rēgīnae* is the possessive noun. All the jewels belong to the queen!

C. Nāvicula nautae pīrātam portat.

This is a longer sentence. It has more parts, but if you think carefully, you will be able to understand the meaning. *Nāvicula* is the subject noun. *Nautae* is the possessive noun. It tells who has the little boat. *Pīrātam* is the direct object noun.

D. Nauta galeās pīrātārum portat.

Nauta is the subject. *Galeās* is the direct object noun. *Pīrātārum* is the possessive noun. It tells who owns the helmets.

E. Fīlia poētae aquam lacūnae postulat.

Fīlia is the subject noun. *Poētae* is the possessive noun. *Aquam* is the direct object noun. *Lacūnae* is the possessive noun which modifies (tells about) the direct object noun.

Lesson Nineteen Exercises

A. Study this new vocabulary. Remember to learn the entire Latin entry for each word.

RO ta, -ae, f.   SE mi ta, -ae, f.   SIL va, -ae, f.

STEL la, -ae, f.   te NE brae, -ārum, f.   TER ra, -ae, f.

TUR ba, -ae, f.   VIL la, -ae, f.   VI a, -ae, f.

B. Underline the subject nouns with a blue crayon. Then circle the direct object nouns with a purple crayon. Next, put a green X on the possessive nouns.

1. Nautae villam poētae appropinquant.

2. Poēta nautās expectābat.

3. Fīlia poētae nautās nōn amat.

4. Famula poētae nautās nōn laudat.

5. Famula fīliam poētae cēlābit.

6. Nautae et poēta villam poētae explōrābunt.

7. Poēta fīliam vocābit.

8. Nautae famulam poētae ōrābunt appropinquāre.

9. Tum (*then*) famula et fīlia nautās appropinquābunt.

10. Nautae fābulam nāviculārum nārrābunt.

C. Write a story about a queen, her palace, and her gems. Remember to use nominative, genitive, and accusative case for the nouns in the story. Write the story in Latin. Do not write it in English first!

_____ ____

_____

_____

_____

_____

_____

D. Write the four principal parts of each verb in your story.

_____

_____

_____

_____

_____

_____

E. Write the noun paradigm for *nauta*.

CASE	SINGULAR	PLURAL
Nominative		
Genitive		
Dative		
Accusative		
Ablative		

Lesson Twenty

We have studied direct object nouns. In English these nouns are found in the predicate and complete (complement) the meaning of the subject and verb. A verb may have more than one complement.

Verbs meaning *give*, *tell*, and *show* (and some others) may have an *indirect object* as well as the direct object. In English the indirect object always comes before the direct object in the sentence and tells *to whom* or *for whom* (or *to what* or *for what*) the action of the verb was done.

In the sentence *John sold the watch*, *John* is the subject; *sold* is the verb; and *watch* is the direct object. If we want to say *to whom* the watch was sold, we might say, "John sold Tim the watch." *Tim* answers the question, "*To whom* did John sell the watch?" *Tim* is the indirect object.

To find the indirect object, ask:
To whom or for whom (to what or for what) was the action done?

Lesson Twenty Exercises

A. Underline the indirect objects with a blue crayon. Put a red X on the direct objects.

1. Mother told Tom the answer.
2. Tom gave Mother a candy bar.
3. Sally gave the baby a toy.
4. Jane was telling the cat a story.
5. Father showed Gilbert the new hammer.
6. Gilbert made Mother a table.
7. Sue will give Sally a book.
8. Fran gave the horse an apple.
9. Tom fed the chickens some oats.
10. Fred shows the boys a truck.

Lesson Twenty-One

Latin is a bit different from English in the way we show indirect objects. Latin is easier, because the direct and indirect objects look different. The direct object is in the accusative case, so it uses *-am* or *-ās* for an ending. But the indirect object uses the *dative* case, so its ending is *-ae* or *-īs*. Review the paradigm chart:

CASE	SINGULAR	PLURAL
Nominative	puella	puellae
Genitive	puellae	puellārum
Dative	puellae	puellīs
Accusative	puellam	puellās
Ablative	puellā	puellīs

The dative singular ending is the same as the genitive singular and the nominative plural endings. Most often we can tell which case is being used by looking carefully at the sentence. Use these hints to help you find the indirect object noun.

1) The dative (indirect object noun) usually comes before the direct object in English and in Latin.

2) The dative case is found with verbs meaning *give*, *tell*, and *show*.

3) When the subject is nominative plural *(-ae)* the verb will end with *-nt*.

The verbs in these sentences are showing, giving, telling verbs which you will learn in this lesson. Look for the indirect object nouns.

A. Famula Annae gemmam dat.

Famula is the subject noun; *Annae* is the indirect object noun; *gemmam* is the direct object noun.

B. Anna amitae gemmam mōnstrat.

Anna is the subject noun, *amitae* is the indirect object noun, and *gemmam* is the direct object noun.

C. Anna famulīs fābulam nārrat.

Anna is the subject noun; *famulīs* is the (plural) indirect object noun; and *fābulam* is the direct object noun.

Lesson Twenty-One Exercises

A. Give yourself a ★ for each part of speech which you can quickly define.

noun

verb

personal pronoun

B. Give yourself a ✓ for each use in the sentence which you can quickly define.

subject noun

direct object noun

indirect object noun

possessive noun

C. Give an example (Latin or English) of the three tenses of verbs which you have learned.

present _____

imperfect _____

future _____

D. Study this new vocabulary. Remember to learn the entire Latin entry for each word.

dō, DA re, DE dī, DA tum[1]

MŌN strō, -āre, -āvī, -ātum

RO gō, -āre, -āvī, -ātum

SPEC tō, -āre, -āvī, -ātum

stō, STĀ re, STE tī, STĀ tum

SER vō, -āre, -āvī, -ātum

---

[1] Dō has no macrons in its stem except in the present tense, first and second persons.

E. Circle the indirect object nouns.

1. Anna fēminae fābulam nārrābat.

2. Anna agricolae pīrātās mōnstrat.

3. Agricola pīrātīs villam nōn dabat.

4. Incolae pīrātae gemmās mōnstrābunt.

5. Pīrātae fēminīs gemmās dabunt.

6. Diana agricolae aquam ōrat. (This verb acts like a *telling* verb.)

7. Agricolae Dianae aquam nōn portant. (This verb acts like a *giving* verb.)

8. Ursa puellīs cūrās dat.

9. Rēgīna agricolae prōvinciam dabit.

10. Agricola rēgīnae bēstiās mōnstrat.

F. Write a short Latin story about a pirate and his small boat.

_____

_____

_____

_____

_____

_____

_____

_____

_____

_____

_____

_____

_____

Lesson Twenty-Two

We have learned many ways to write sentences with nouns and verbs. But there are other kinds of words which make our writing even more interesting. An *adjective* tells *which one, what kind, how many* about a noun. Look at the difference in these sentences.

A. The boy wants balls.

B. The smiling, happy boy wants three big, blue, bouncy balls.

The adjectives we added make the second sentence much more exciting. This sentence gives us a more exact picture of the boy and the balls. Now we know exactly which boy, what kind of boy, how many balls he wants, and what kind of balls they are.

An adjective tells
which one, what kind, how many about a noun.

Lesson Twenty-Two Exercises

A. Underline the adjectives in this story.

Samson was a strong young man. One hot, sunny day when he was walking on a long, dusty road, a roaring young lion came after him. He killed the fierce lion. After many days, Samson traveled the same road. He saw the dead lion. There were many honeybees in it. Samson ate some delicious honey.

Later, Samson used the dead lion and the honeybees to tell a hard riddle about sweet food coming from a strong beast.

B. Add adjectives to make these sentences more interesting and exact.

1. The king had a palace.

_____

2. The bird ate a spider.

_____

3. The children like sandwiches.

_____

4. The bug was a ladybug.

_____

5. The house looked like a store.

_____

6. The box had letters on it.

_____

Lesson Twenty-Three

Of course Latin has adjectives, too. In Latin it is easy to tell which noun an adjective modifies (describes). An adjective agrees with the noun it modifies in gender, number, and case. That is, it will have a masculine, feminine, or neuter declension ending; it will be singular or plural; and it will be nominative, genitive, dative, accusative, or ablative—the same as the noun it modifies.

In the vocabulary listing, there will be three forms. These are nominative singular for the masculine, feminine, and neuter genders. Adjectives are always listed in this order. For example: *bonus, bona, bonum* is the adjective to describe something good. Study the three forms. We will use the middle form to modify the feminine nouns we have learned.

A Latin adjective often follows its noun. If there are two adjectives, one may come before the noun and one after the noun, or they may be joined by *et* (and). An adjective which tells how big or how many usually comes before the noun it modifies. The best way to tell which noun an adjective is modifying is to look for the case ending!

This is the paradigm we would use to write sentences about a good servant:

famula bona	famulae bonae
famulae bonae	famulārum bonārum
famulae bonae	famulīs bonīs
famulam bonam	famulās bonās
famulā bonā	famulīs bonīs

These sentences show adjective-noun pairs.

A. Parva puella amitam bonam amat.

Subject: *parva puella*

Direct Object: *amitam bonam*

B. Fēmina bona parvae puellae gemmam novam dat.

Subject: *fēmina bona*

Indirect Object: *parvae puellae*

Direct Object: *gemmam novam*

C. Famula bona fēminae pulchrae parvae puellae gemmam novam dat.

Subject: *famula bona*

Possessive: *fēminae pulchrae*

Indirect Object: *parvae puellae*

Direct Object: *gemmam novam*

In this sentence it is important to remember that the genitive noun usually comes directly after the noun it possesses and the indirect object comes before the direct object.

Lesson Twenty-Three Exercises

A. Study the three forms for these adjectives. We will be using the middle form.

BO nus, BO na, BO num

FĪ dus, FĪ da, FĪ dum

FE rus, FE ra, FE rum

LAE tus, LAE ta, LAE tum

6 feet

LON gus, LON ga, LON gum

MAG nus, MAG na, MAG num

MUL tus, MUL ta, MUL tum   PAR vus, PAR va, PAR vum

PRĪ mus, PRĪ ma, PRĪ mum   PUL cher, PUL chra, PUL chrum

qui Ē tus, qui Ē ta, qui Ē tum   RAU cus, RAU ca, RAU cum

B. Make the adjective agree in gender, number, and case with the noun it modifies. In this exercise, all the nouns are feminine in gender.

1. Fēmina bon_____ fīliam parv_____ vocat.

2. Parv_____ puella fīlia bon_____ est.

3. Famulae fīd_____ mult_____ gemmās cēlābant.

4. Bēstia fer_____ puellam laet_____ appropinquat.

5. Amitae quiēt_____ famulās laet_____ amant.

6. Rēgīna prīm_____ corōnam pulchr_____ portābit.

7. Famula laet_____ parv_____ casam habitat.

8. Magn_____ turba long_____ paenīnsulam explorat.

9. Parv_____ ursae clamant.

10. Nauta nāviculam pulchr_____ nāvigābat.

11. Rēgīnae bon_____ magn_____ rēgiās habitant.

12. Bēstiās fer_____ nōn amāmus.

C. Say the chant for these noun-adjective pairs.

multa pecūnia   parva cūra   bēstia rauca

D. Say the conjugation, present, imperfect, and future for these verbs.

cēlō   dō   laudō   amō

E. Read these sentences. Draw a picture or write an English sentence to show the meaning.

1. Fēmina bona fīliam parvam vocat.

2. Famulae fīdae multās gemmās cēlābant.

3. Bēstia fera puellam laetam appropinquat.

Lesson Twenty-Four

Sometimes adjectives are used with linking verbs. An adjective in the predicate which describes the subject noun after a linking verb is called the predicate adjective. Here are some sentences which contain predicate adjectives:

A. The dog is big.

B. The girl is glad.

C. They are happy.

A. Underline the predicate adjective.

1. The puppy was tired.

2. The baby is hungry.

3. The elephant is huge.

4. The flowers are beautiful.

5. Trucks are noisy.

6. Tomorrow will be sunny.

7. Grass is green.

Lesson Twenty-Five

In Latin a predicate adjective is like any other adjective. It agrees with the noun it modifies in gender, number, and case. Very often it will be next to the noun it modifies in the sentence. Here are some sentences which have predicate adjectives.

A. Famula fīda est.

B. Fīgūra magna est.

C. Bēstiae ferae sunt.

D. Pulchra est.

E. Laetae sumus.

Lesson Twenty-Five Exercises

A. Identify the predicate adjective.

1. Undae magnae sunt.

2. Via longa est.

3. Stella parva est.

4. Ursa fera est.

5. Rēgīna quiēta est.

6. Famulae pulchrae sunt.

7. Coma longa est.

8. Fāma bona est.

9. Fenestrae parvae sunt.

10. Rēgia magna est.

B. Write PN or PA for the underlined words.

1. Amita <u>quiēta</u> est.

2. Flamma <u>stella</u> est.

3. Aqua <u>bona</u> est.

4. Bēstiae <u>ferae</u> sunt.

5. <u>Raucae</u> nōn sumus. [Assume that ladies are speaking.]

Lesson Twenty-Six

Adjectives make a sentence interesting by describing nouns. Another way to make a sentence interesting is by using a *prepositional phrase*. A prepositional phrase is a group of words that begins with a preposition and contains a noun which is the object of the preposition. A preposition is a short word which tells the position of a noun or pronoun (the object of the preposition) in relation to another word in the sentence.

These sentences tell the relationship between the box (the object of the preposition) and the frog. The noun or pronoun after the preposition is the object of the preposition.

A. The frog is *in* the box.

B. The frog is *under* the box.

C. The frog is *behind* the box.

Lesson Twenty-Six Exercises

A. Underline all the prepositional phrases.

Early Romans lived in one-room houses. This large room had a hole in the roof for light and air. A basin in the floor below this hole caught rain water. Later, rooms were added around the sides of the building.

Still later, wealthy people built open courts with gardens and sometimes with fountains. To save on plumbing, the kitchen was near the bathroom, usually at the rear of the open court. Fancy houses sometimes had rooms on a second level. These rooms had openings to the court, but there was no glass in these "windows."

Lesson Twenty-Seven

We have learned the uses of four cases in our noun paradigm. The nominative case is used for the subject noun or the predicate nominative. The genitive case shows possession. The dative case shows the indirect object, to whom or for whom the action of the verb was done. The accusative case shows the direct object, who or what received the action of the verb.

The *ablative* case is used to show prepositional relationships. A. The *ablative of means* tells what was used to do an action. *Parvā nāviculā* shows that "by means of a small boat," "with a small boat," "by a small boat," something was done.

Parvā nāviculā nauta rēgīnam portat.

In this sentence the sailor is using a small boat to carry the queen. *Parvā nāviculā* tells *how?* or *by what means?* he is doing the action.

The *ablative of means*
answers the questions how?, by what means?,
with what? the action is done.

Agricola bēstiam hastā necat.

In this sentence the farmer is killing the beast with a spear. *Hastā* tells *how?* or *with what?* the farmer does the action.

   B. The *ablative of time* tells when (at what time, or within what period of time) an action was done. *Prīmā hōrā* tells that something was done at the first hour or during (in or within) the first hour.

   Unā (one) hōrā puella sēmitam ambulābit.

The girl will walk the path in one hour or within one hour. The other sentences in the story would help us to understand whether to use *in* or *within*.

   Prīmā hōrā bēstia clamat.

In (or during) the first hour the beast shouts.

The *ablative of time* answers the questions when? or within what time? the action is done.

Lesson Twenty-Seven Exercises

A. Study the new vocabulary.

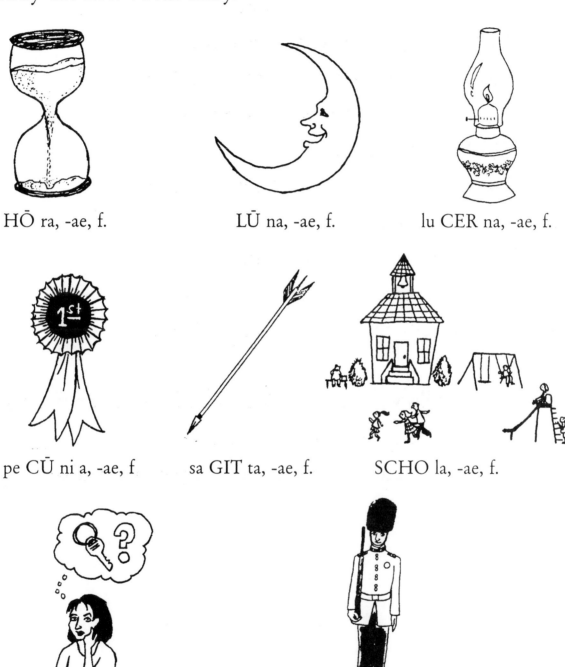

HŌ ra, -ae, f.

LŪ na, -ae, f.

lu CER na, -ae, f.

pe CŪ ni a, -ae, f

sa GIT ta, -ae, f.

SCHO la, -ae, f.

dē SI de rō, -āre, -āvī, -ātum

VI gi lō, -āre, -āvī, -ātum

B. Underline the ablative nouns. Tell whether they are ablative of means (M) or ablative of time when (T).

1. Sagittā incola bēstiam necābit.

2. Fēmina sēmitam lucernā spectābat.

3. Prīmā hōrā nautae nāviculam nāvigābunt.

4. Puella laeta famulam pecūniā laudat.

5. Unā hōrā laeta sumus.

6. Rēgīna gemmās pulchrās latebrā cēlābat.

7. Lucernā vigilō.

8. Famula fīliam fābulā occupat.

9. Incolae paenīnsulam lūnā explorābant.

10. Prīmā stellā agricolae nōn ambulābunt.

C. Read the following sentences. Draw pictures or write a good English sentence to show the meaning.

1. Nautae multam pecūniam nāviculā parvā portābant.

2. Rēgīna bona parvam fīliam laetam amat.

3. Famula fīda multās puellās lucernā vigilat.

4. Bēstiae raucae agricolam appropinquābant.

5. Famulae fīdae et puella quiēta rēgiam pulchram habitābunt.

6. Fēmina laeta et fīlia parva sēmitam longam lūnā ambulant.

Lesson Twenty-Eight

The accusative case and the ablative case have another use. It is a very important use and one which will give us great variety in writing sentences.

Latin has prepositions (short words which tell the position of a noun or pronoun in relation to another word in the sentence). The nouns which come after these prepositions are called the *objects of the preposition*. The noun case of these objects will be accusative or ablative, depending on which preposition is used. When we learn the preposition, it is very important to learn the case it governs (controls).

For example, *in* used with the accusative case means *into*, but when it is used with the ablative case it means *in* or *on*. It is very important to look carefully at the noun cases to see the meaning of the sentence.

Agricola in silvā ambulat means something different from *agricola in silvam ambulat*. The first sentence gives a picture of the farmer walking *in* a forest. The second sentence gives a picture of the farmer going *into* the forest.

The accusative case sometimes carries the idea of motion (toward, into, through) while the ablative case conveys the idea of confinement or leaving (in, under, on, away from, out of).

Here is a list of common prepositions and their meanings.

ā, ab (ablative) *away from*

ad (accusative) *to, toward*

circum (accusative) *around*

cum (ablative) *with*

dē (ablative) *concerning, about*

ē, ex (ablative) *away from*

in (accusative) *into*

in (ablative) *in, on*

inter (accusative) *between, among*

per (accusative) *through*

post (accusative) *after, behind*

prō (ablative) *in front of*

prope (accusative) *near*

Lesson Twenty-Eight Exercises

A. Write the Latin prepositional phrase which shows the meaning of these English phrases.

1. on the path _____

2. through the forest _____

3. around the palace _____

4. behind the cottages _____

5. in front of the hiding place _____

_____

6. toward the fierce beast _____

7. near the large beaches _____

8. about the happy girls _____

9. with a quiet maid _____

10. among the noisy beasts _____

_____

11. away from the water in the pool _____

_____

12. in (during) the first story _____

_____

B. Using phrases you created in Exercise A, write a Latin story. Remember to have all your adjectives agree in gender, number, and case with the nouns they modify.

_____

_____

_____

_____

_____

_____

_____

_____

_____

_____

_____

_____

_____

_____

_____

_____

_____

_____

_____

Iūlia—Passage 1

Iūlia puella parva est. Prope ōram maritimam habitat. Britannia est Iūliae patria. Puellae Britannicae quoque ōram maritimam amant. Nautās quoque amant puellae Britannicae. Iūlia est fīlia agricolae et casam parvam habitat. Sed Iūlia ōram maritimam et nautās amat. Nautae quoque Iūlia amant. Saepe prope ōram maritimam Iūlia ambulat. Fīliae nautārum cum Iūliā ambulant, et prope ōram maritimam saltant. Multae rosae sunt prope casam Iūliae. Rosīs aquam dat Iūlia. Saepe Iūlia rosās nautīs dat. Agricola Iūliam nōn culpat sed laudat, quod rosās pulchrās nautīs dat. Rubrae et albae sunt rosae. Saepe Iūlia ad casās nautārum rosās pulchrās portat. Nautae puellam parvam laudant.

---

albus, alba, album—white
Britannia, -ae, f.—Britain
Britannicus, -a, -um—British
culpō, -āre, -āvī, -ātum—to place blame
multus, -a, -um—much, many
ōra maritima—seashore

quoque—also
rosa, -ae, f.—rose
ruber, rubra, rubrum—red
saepe—often
saltō, -āre, -āvī, ātum—to dance
sed—but

Iūlia—Passage 2

Ad casam Iūliae pīrāta vēnit. Rubra est tunica pīrātae, splendidae sunt galea et hasta. Iūlia prope portam casae stat et pīrātam spectat; hastam pīrātae et galeam et tunicam rubram amat et laudat. Pīrāta quoque Iūliam et casam et rosās laudat. "O Iūlia," inquit, "pulchra es puella et pulchrae sunt rosae tuae. Nāvicula mea pulchra est. Alta est prōra nāviculae meae. In extrēmā nāviculā stō et nāviculam gubernō. Alba est nāvicula mea; nunc prope ōram maritimam stat." Tum Iūlia cum pīrātā ad ōram maritimam ambulat et nāviculam albam spectat. Iūlia et pīrāta prōram nāviculae multīs rosīs ornant. Subitō pīrāta puellam in nāviculam iactat. Multae sunt lacrimae puellae, sed frustrā—pīrāta in extrēmā nāviculā stat et nāviculam gubernat.

altus, alta, altum—high, deep
extrēmus, -a, -um—outermost, farthest
frūstrā—in vain
gubernō, -āre, -āvī, -ātum—to steer a ship
iactō, -āre, -āvī, -ātum—to throw, to hurl
inquit—he says
lacrima, -ae, f.—tear (crying)
meus, mea, meum—my

nunc—now
ornō, -āre, -āvī, -ātum—decorate
prōra, -ae, f.—the prow of a ship
subitō—suddenly
tunica, -ae, f.—tunic
tum—then
tuus, tua, tuum—your (s.)
vēnit—he comes

Answer in Latin.

1. Ubi (where) vēnit pīrāta?

2. Quae (what) portat pīrāta?

3. Ubi Iūlia stat?

4. Quae Iūlia laudat?

5. Ubi stat nāvicula alba?

6. Ubi pīrāta iactat puellam?

7. Estne puella laeta?

Appendix A

Lesson Seven Practice Sentences

15. Appropinquātis.

16. Labōrant.

17. Fīliae vocant.

18. Amitae amant.

19. Incolae clamant.

20. Fēminae vocant.

21. Bēstiae clamant.

22. Fīlia et amita appropinquant. *(et = and)*

23. Agricolae et fēminae ambulant.

24. Incola et agricolae labōrant.

25. Amita ambulat et appropinquō.

26. Bēstiae appropinquant et incolae clamant!

27. Amāmus vocāre.

Imperfect Tense Practice Sentences

15. Fīliae errābant.

16. Amitae amābant.

17. Incolae clamābant.

18. Fēminae vocābant.

19. Bēstiae clamābant.

20. Fīlia et amita appropinquābant.

Challenge:

21. Fēminae amābant ambulāre.

22. Incola et agricolae iuvābant labōrāre.

23. Amita ambulābat et appropinquābam.

24. Bēstiae cēlābant et incola explōrābat!

25. Navigābātis.

26. Amābāmus errāre.

Future Tense Practice Sentences

15. Expectābō.

16. Fēmina et nauta explōrābunt.

17. Habitābis.

18. Agricola iuvābit.

19. Laudābit.

20. Bēstiae mutābunt.

21. Nārrābimus.

22. Nauta navigābit.

23. Vocābitis.

24. Amita et fīlia ambulābunt.

Challenge:

25. Fēminae amābunt ambulāre.

26. Incola et agricolae iuvābunt labōrāre.

27. Amita ambulābit et appropinquābō.

28. Bēstiae celābunt et incola explōrābit!

29. Amābimus errāre.

30. Pīrātae appropinquābunt oppugnāre.

Appendix B

Adjective Declension

SINGULAR

MASCULINE	FEMININE	NEUTER
bonus	bona	bonum
bonī	bonnae	bonī
bonō	bonae	bonō
bonum	bonam	bonum
bonō	bonā	bonō

PLURAL

bonī	bonae	bona
bonōrum	bonārum	bonōrum
bonīs	bonīs	bonīs
bonōs	bonās	bona
bonīs	bonīs	bonīs

Appendix   C

Objectives

Upon completion of this text the student should be able to do the following tasks in Latin and in English.

1. Identify a noun (common and proper) and tell its use in a sentence as a subject, predicate nominative, direct object, indirect object, or object of a preposition.

2. Identify an adjective and the noun it modifies.

3. Identify a personal pronoun and use it as the subject of a verb.

4. Recognize possessive pronouns and their use as adjectives.

5. Recognize *a, an,* and *the* as articles.

6. Recognize linking verbs and give their tense (present, imperfect, or future).

7. Recognize action verbs with their helping verbs and give their tense (present, imperfect, or future).

8. Identify prepositions and prepositional phrases.

The student should be able to do the following tasks in Latin.

10. Read simple Latin selections for enjoyment.

11. Decline any first declension noun.

12. Conjugate any first conjugation verb in the present, imperfect, and future tenses.

13. Have a working Latin vocabulary of about 125 words.

Vocabulary-Nouns

A

a GRI co la, -ae, m.,	farmer
A mi ta, -ae, f.,	aunt
A qua, -ae, f.,	water
Ā ra, -ae, f.,	altar
au DĀ ci a, -ae, f.,	boldness
a vā RI ti a, -ae, f.,	greed

B

be ne vo LEN ti a, -ae, f.,	favor, good will
BĒS ti a, -ae, f.,	wild beast

C

CA sa, -ae, f.,	house, cottage
co RŌ na, -ae, f.,	crown
con STAN ti a, -ae, f.,	constancy, steadfastness
CO ma, -ae, f.,	hair
CŌ pi a, -ae, f.,	supply, abundance
CŪ ra, -ae, f.,	care, worry

D

DE a, -ae, f.,	goddess

F

FA mu la, -ae, f.,	a female servant, handmaid
FĀ bu la, -ae, f.,	story, tale, fable
FĀ ma, -ae, f.,	fame, talk, rumor, report
fe NES tra, -ae, f.,	window
FĒ mi na, -ae, f.,	woman
fi GŪ ra, -ae, f.,	shape, figure
FĪ li a, -ae, f.,	daughter
FLAM ma, -ae, f.,	flame

G

GA le a, -ae, f.,   helmet
GEM ma, -ae, f.,   gem, jewel

H

ha RE na, -ae, f.,   beach, sand
HAS ta, -ae, f.,   spear
HER ba, -ae, f.,   herb, plant
HO ra, -ae, f.,   hour

I

IN co la, -ae, m.,   inhabitant, resident, settler
ĪN su la, -ae, f.,   island
IĀ nu a, -ae, f.,   door

L

la CŪ na, -ae, f.,   pool, pond
la TE bra, - ae, f.,   hiding place, lair, hideout
LIN gua, -ae, f.,   tongue, language
LIT te ra, -ae, f.,   letter (of the alphabet)
LIT te rae, -ārum, f. pl.   letter (correspondence)
lu CER na, -ae, f.,   lantern, lamp
LŪ na, -ae, f.,   moon

M

MEN sa, -ae, f.,   table
mi se ri COR di a, - ae, f.,   pity, mercy

N

nā VI cu la, -ae, f.,   small ship or boat
NAU ta, -ae, in.,   sailor
NYM pha, -ae, f.,   nymph

O

Ō ra, -ae, f.,   coast, shore

P

pae NĪN su la, -ae, f.,	peninsula
pe CŪ ni a, -ae, f.,	money, reward
pī RĀ ta, -ae, f.,	pirate
pic TŪ ra, -ae, f.,	picture
po Ē ta, -se, m.,	poet
POE na, -ae, f.,	penalty, punishment
prō VIN ci a, -ae, f.,	province
pu EL la, -ae, f.,	girl

R

rē GĪ na, -ae, f.,	queen
RĒ gi a, -ae, f.,	palace, royal residence
RĪ pa, -ae, f.,	bank (of a river)
RO ta, -ae, f.,	wheel

S

sa GIT ta, -ae, f.,	arrow
sa pi EN ti a, -ae, f.,	wisdom
SCHO la, -ae, f.,	school
SE mi ta, -ae, f.,	path
SIL va, -ae, f.,	forest, wood
STEL la, -ae, f.,	star

T

te NE brae, -ārum, f. pl.,	shadows, darkness
TER ra, -ae, f.,	land, earth, ground
TUR ba, -ae, f.,	crowd, throng, mob

U

UM bra, -ae, f.,	shade, ghost
UN da, -ae, f.,	wave
UR sa, -ae, f.,	bear

V

VIL la, -ae, f.,	villa, house
VI a, -ae, f.,	street, road, highway, way
VĪ ta, -ae, f.,	life

Vocabulary–Adjectives

A

apertus, aperta, apertum   open

B

bonus, bona, bonum   good

D

dēnsus, dēnsa, dēnsum   thick, dense

F

ferus, fera, ferum   fierce
fīdus, fīda, fīdum   faithful

G

grātus, grāta, grātum   pleasing

L

laetus, laeta, laetum   happy, glad
līberus, lībera, līberum   free
longus, longa, longum   long

M

malus, mala, malum   bad, evil, wicked
magnus, magna, magnum   great, large
multus, multa, multum   many, much

P

parvus, parva, parvum   small, little
prīmus, prīma, prīmum   first
pulcher, pulchra, pulchrum   beautiful
perterritus, territa, territum   frightened

Q

quiētus, quiēta, quiētum   quiet

R

raucus, rauca, raucum   noisy, raucous

S

sōlus, sōla, sōlum   alone, only

Vocabulary–Verbs

A

AC cu sō, -āre, -āvī, -ātum	to accuse, to blame
A gi tō, -āre, -āvī, -ātum	to drive, to arouse, to disturb
AM bu lō, -āre, -āvī, -ātum	to walk
A mō, -āre, -āvī, -ātum	to love
ap pro PIN quō, -āre, -āvī, -ātum	to approach, to draw near

C

CĒ lō, -āre, -āvī, -ātum	to hide, to conceal
CLA mō, - āre, -āvī, -ātum	to shout, to cry out
con CI li ō, -āre, - āvī, -ātum	to win over
con SER vō, -āre, -āvī, - ātum	to save, to preserve
con VO cō, -āre, -āvī, -ātum	to call together

D

dē MON strō, -āre, -āvī, -ātum	to point out, to show
dē SĪ de rō, -āre, -āvī, -ātum	to desire, to want
dō, DA re, DE dī, DA tum	to give

E

ER rō, -āre, -āvī, -ātum	to err, to wander, to be mistaken
ex PEC tō, -āre, -āvī, -ātum	to expect, to wait for
ex PLO rō, - āre, -āvī, -ātum	to explore
ē VO cō, -āre, - āvī, -ātum	to evoke, to call forth

H

HA bi tō, -āre, -āvī, -ātum	to dwell, to live in, to inhabit

I

IU vō, iuvāre, iūvī, iūtum	to help, to aid

L

LA bō rō, -āre, -āvī, -ātum	to work
LAU dō, -āre, -āvī, -ātum	to praise

M

MAN dō, -āre, -āvī, -ātum   to entrust
MŌN strō, -āre, -āvī, -ātum   to show, to point out
MU tō, -āre, -āvī, -ātum   to change, to alter

N

NĀR rō, -āre, -āvī, -ātum   to tell
NĀ vi gō, -āre, -āvī, -ātum   to sail
NE cō, -āre, -āvī, -ātum   to kill
NŌ mi nō, -āre, -āvī, -ātum   to name, to call

O

OC cu pō, -āre, -āvī, -ātum   to seize, to occupy
Ō rō, -āre, -āvī, -ātum   to ask for
op PUG nō, -āre, -āvī, -ātum   to attack

P

POR tō, -āre, -āvī, -ātum   to carry
POS tu lō, -āre, -āvī, -ātum   to demand
PRO pe rō, -āre, -āvī, -ātum   to hasten, to hurry
PUG nō, -āre, -āvī, -ātum   to fight

R

re CŪ sō, -āre, -āvī, -ātum   to refuse
RO gō, -āre, -āvī, -ātum   to ask

S

SER vō, -āre, -āvī, -ātum   to save, to keep
SPEC tō, -āre, -āvī, -ātum   to look at, to watch
stō, STĀ re, STE tī, STĀ tum   to stand
sum, ES se, FU ī, fu TŪ rus   to be

T

TAR dō, -āre, -āvī, -ātum   to slow down, to delay
TEM ptō, -āre, -āvī, -ātum   to try, to attempt

V

VI gi lō, -āre, -āvī, -ātum	to be on guard, to stand watch
VĪ tō, -āre, -āvī, -ātum	to avoid, to shun
VO cō, -āre, -āvī, -ātum	to call
VO lō, -āre, -āvī, -ātum	to fly
VUL ne rō, -āre, -āvī, -ātum	to wound